2022 Best Mutual Funds

King Kovacs

Copyright©2023 All rights reserved.

Do not reproduce or copy any of the data herein.

KDP Amazon published.

Dedication

The book is dedicated to my beautiful wife, Claire. Her confidence, encouragement and devotion to the Author helped establish the successful pensions that are based on his principals found in King Kovacs' book.

Acknowledgment

Appreciation is extended to Amazon Kindle Direct Publishing for publishing the Kindle, Paperback, and Hard cover of 2022 Best Mutual Funds. In addition, thank you to the technical support team for assisting the Author in developing of this book. Also, thanks to the internet financial websites for providing mutual fund data.

CONTENTS

Dedication iii

Acknowledgment iv

Prologue viii

Introduction: 1

Retirement Prosperity 2

2022 Best Mutual Funds 13

Alternative Currency Strategy 15

Alternative Long/Short Equity 19

Alternative Managed Futures 23

Equity Income 27

Equity Leverage 31

Financial Service 35

Flexible Portfolio 39

Global Multi-Cap Value 43

Global Small-Cap Core 47

Health/Biotechnology 51

v

Large-Cap Value 55

Mid-Cap Core 59

Mid-Cap Growth 63

Mid-Cap Value 67

Mixed-Asset: Target Allocation Growth 71

Mixed-Asset: Target Allocation Moderate 75

Multi-Cap Core 79

Multi-Cap Growth 83

Multi-Cap Value 87

Sector: Natural Resources 91

Small-Cap Core 95

Small-Cap Growth 99

Small-Cap Value 103

Utility 107

Multi-Cap Value 111

Sector: Natural Resources 116

Small-Cap Core 121

Small-Cap Growth 126

Small-Cap Value 131

Utility 136

Self-Directed Retirement Investing 141

Individual Retirement Account 143

Mutual Fund Investing 146

Prologue

There are twenty-three reports of mutual fund moneymakers. Each mutual fund's performance rank is in the top 10% of the investment category served.

An investment model in the Retirement Prosperity section reveals the success of building a growing and wealthy portfolio. The model analyzes an IRA mutual fund investment for 12 years.

The financial information is accurate, dependable, and thorough. The author does not assume and, at this moment, refuses liability for possible human error. There are no guarantees of future results. The material and data presented in this paperback are for informational purposes only.

Introduction:

Knowing and understanding the fundamentals of the book helps achieve goals of prosperity for retirement and/or savings portfolios. The verifiable data consist of money-making investments based on annual performance returns.

King Kovacs (Mutual Fund Analyst & Author) formed Mutual Interest Data Service, Ltd. in 1999 to find moneymakers for investments. To accomplish this challenging task, the author had to extensively screen and analyze thousands of mutual funds to achieve the objective.

King Kovacs

Retirement Prosperity

Here is an excellent example of how to accumulate retirement wealth. This investment model covers ten years (2010 through 2022). To acquire this type of financial success, you must commit to Making maximum annual IRA investments and reinvesting all distributions. The investments started on June 1,2010.

The bottom line is, as of December 30, 2022, the accumulated wealth is $165,514.18. Here are the facts: The Mutual Fund is Oakmark I– OAKMX and the Category is Multi-Cap Core.

June 1, 2010

IRA Purchase: $6,000

Net Asset Value: $36.91

Total Shares Purchased: 162.5576

December 17, 2010

Distribution: $.25 $40.64

Shares Reinvested: 1.0098Total Shares Owned: 163.5674

December 31, 2010

Net Asset Value: $41.30

Total Shares Owned: 163.5674

2022 Best Mutual Funds

IRA Portfolio Value: $6,755.33

June 1, 2011
IRA Purchased: $6,000
Net Asset Value: $43.74
Total Shares Purchased: 137.1742

December 19, 2011
Distribution: $.35 $105.26
Shares Reinvested: 2.6341
Total Shares Owned: 303.3757

December 30, 2011
Net Asset Value: $41.69
Total Shares Owned: 303.3757
Portfolio Value: $12,647.73 5.40%

June 1, 2012
IRA Purchased: $6,000
Net Asset Value: $42.86
Total Shares Purchased: 140.0887

December 18, 2012

Distribution: $1.88 $903.12

Shares Reinvested: 19.3595

Total Shares Owned: 462.8239

December 31, 2012

Net Asset Value: $48.53

Total Shares Owned: 462.8239

IRA Portfolio Value: $22,460.84

June 1, 2013

IRA Purchased: $6,500

Net Asset Value: $57.16

Total Shares Purchased: 113.716

December 19, 2013

Distribution: $3.00 $1,840

Shares Reinvested: 27.1138

Total Shares Owned: 603.6536

December 31, 2013

2022 Best Mutual Funds

Net Asset Value: $62.09

Total Shares Owned: 603.653

IRA Portfolio Value: $37,480.85

June 1, 2014

IRA Purchase: $6,500

Net Asset Value: $66.67

Total Shares Purchased: 97.4951

December 18, 2014

Distribution: $4.55 $3,190

Shares Reinvested: 48.2636

Total Shares Owned: 749.4123

December 31, 2014

Net Asset Value: $66.38

Total Shares Owned: 749.4123

IRA Portfolio Value: $49,745.99

June 1, 2015

IRA Purchase: $6,500

Net Asset Value: $67.66

King Kovacs

Total Shares Purchased: 96.0686

December 17, 2015

Distribution: $.90 $760.93

Shares Reinvested: 12.1148

Total Shares Owned: 857.5957

December 31, 2015

Net Asset Value: $62.86

Total Shares Owned: 857.5957

IRA Portfolio Value: $53,908.47

June 1, 2016

IRA Purchase: $6,500

Net Asset Value: $64.88

Total Shares Purchased: 100.1850

November 28, 2016

Distribution: $1.87 $1603

Shares Reinvested: 22.7250

Total Shares Owned: 980.5057

2022 Best Mutual Funds

December 30, 2016

Net Asset Value: $72.48

Total Shares Owned: 980.5057

IRA Portfolio Value: $71,067.05

June 1, 2017

IRA Purchase: $6,500

Net Asset Value: $78.58

Total Shares Purchased: 82.7182

December 14, 2017

Distribution: $3.42 $3636

Shares Reinvested: 46.87

Total Shares Owned: 1110.09

December 29, 2017

Net Asset Value: $84.33

Total Shares Owned: 1110.09

IRA Portfolio Value: $93,614.22

King Kovacs

June 1, 2018

IRA Purchase: $6,500

Net Asset Value: $85.37

Total Shares Purchased: 76.1392

December 13, 2018

Distribution: $5.55 $658

Shares Reinvested: $71.50

Total Shares Owned: 1278.3071

December 29, 2018

Net Asset Value: $68.29

Total Shares Owned: 1278.3071

IRA Portfolio Value: $87,295.59

June 3, 2019

IRA Purchase: $6,500

Net Asset Value: $73.60

Total Shares Purchased: 88.3152

2022 Best Mutual Funds

December 12, 2019

Distribution: $6.66 $9101.70

Shares Reinvested: 115.4306

Total Shares Owned: 1482.0529

December 31, 2019

Net Asset Value: $79.96

Total Shares Owned: 1482.0529

IRA Portfolio Value: $118,504.95

June 18, 2020

IRA Purchase: $6,500

Net Asset Value: $68.51

Total Shares Purchased: 94.8766

December 10, 2020

Net Asset Value $88.85

Distribution: $.15 $236.54

Shares Reinvested: 2.6622

Total Shares Owned: 1579.5917

King Kovacs

December 31, 2020

Net Asset Value: $94.23

Total Shares Owned: 1579.5917

IRA Portfolio: $148,844.92

December 16, 2021

Net Asset Value: $119.17

Distribution: $1.75

Shares Reinvested: 23.4823

Total Shares Owned: 1603.074

December 31, 2021

Net Asset Value: $119.17

Total Shares Owned: 1603.074

IRA Portfolio: $191,038.32

December 16, 2022

Net Asset Value: $102.56

Distribution: $.94 $1,506.89

Shares Reinvested: 14.697

Total Shares Owned: 1617.771

2022 Best Mutual Funds

December 30, 2022

Net Asset Value: $102.31

IRA Portfolio: $165,514.18

Total Prosperity

IRA Investments:	$70,000.00
Income Reinvested:	$29,505.97
Dollar-Cost Averaging:	$66,008.21

Total IRA Portfolio:	$165,514.18
Investment Return:	$95,514.18
12-Year Annualized Return:	11.37%

2022 Best Mutual Funds

Here are 23 mutual fund reports. There is no guarantee of completeness or accuracy of the researched mutual fund data* based on the last market closing date in December of each year.

You should examine the five years of returns and the annualized returns of each mutual fund. This valuable information reveals the actual performance for every year.

In addition, the annualized returns show each investment's average performance and ranking. The fund's rank is based on performance within the total funds in the mutual fund category.

There are no guarantees of future results. Always contact the mutual fund and read the prospectus.

*Source:Finance.Yahoo.com, MarketWatch.com, and WSJ.com

Alternative Currency Strategy 8%

Alternative Long/Short Equity 4%

Alternative Managed Futures 3%

Equity Income 6%

Equity Leverage 3%

Financial Services 4%

Flexible Portfolio 1%

Global Multi-Cap Value 3%

Global Small/Mid-Cap 2%

Health & Biotechnology 1%

Large-Cap Value 1%

Mid-Cap Core 7%

Mid-Cap Growth 1%

Mid-Cap Value 6%

Mixed-Asset Target: Growth 2%

Mixed-Asset Target: Moderate 1%

Multi-Cap Core 2%

Multi-Cap Growth 1%

Multi-Cap Value 1%

Natural Resources 8%

Small-Cap Core 1%

Small-Cap Growth 1%

Small-Cap Value 3%

Utility 4%

Percent represents individual mutual fund rank in the category.

Alternative Currency Strategy

Investment Policy: The Fund seeks daily investment results, before fees and expenses, that correspond to the daily performance of the U.S. Dollar Index. The fund takes positions in financial instruments that, in combination, should have similar daily return characteristics as the U.S. Dollar Index.

Rising U.S. Dollar Pro Fund - RDPIX

888-776-3637

www.profunds.com

ProFunds

3435 Stelzler Road

Columbus, OH 43219

December 30, 2022, Performance:

NAV: $29.55

Return: 7.87%

Investment Rank: 8%

FUND DETAILS:

Open to all investors

Profile Style: Alternative Currency Strategy

King Kovacs

Risk: Average

Minimum Investment Purchase: $15,000

Maximum Front End Sales: no load

Net Expense Ratio: 1.78%

Inception Date: February 17, 2005

Number of Years of Gains: 8

Number of Years of Losses: 9

TOTAL NET ASSETS: $31.90 million

NET ASSET ALLOCATION:

U.S. Equity: 0%

Non–U.S. Equity: 0%

Fixed Income: 0%

Other: 0%

Cash: 100%

Non-Classified: 0%

FIVE-YEAR RETURNS:

Year: 2022

Net Asset Value: $29.55 5.54%

Dividend Distribution: $0.65 2.33%

2022 Best Mutual Funds

Total Return: 7.87%

Year: 2021

Net Asset Value: $28.00 4.67%

Dividend Distribution: $0.00

Total Return: 4.67%

Year: 2020

Net Asset Value: $26.75 -8.08%

Dividend Distribution: $0.00

Total Return: -8.08%

Year: 2019

Net Asset Value: $29.10 2.14%

Dividend Distribution $0.14 0.49%

Total Return: 2.63%

Year: 2018

Net Asset Value: $28.49 5.56%

Dividend Distribution: $0.06 0.22%

Total Return: 5.78%

INVESTMENT RETURNS:

1-year Return: 7.87%

average category: -16.30%

investment rank: 8%

3-year Return: 1.49%

average category: -1.32%

investment rank: 20%

5-year Return: 2.57%

average category: -0.83%

investment rank: 15%

10-year Return: 1.84%

average category: -1.23

investment rank: 11%

3, 5, and 10-year Return annualized

$$$$$

Alternative Long/Short Equity

Investment Policy: The fund seeks to provide long-term capital appreciation, emphasizing protecting capital during unfavorable market conditions. Based on historical evidence, the Manager believes that market return/risk characteristics differ significantly across market conditions.

Hussman Strategic Growth Fund - HSGFX

800-487-7626

www.hussmanfunds.com

Hussman Investment Trust

5136 Dorsey Hall Drive

Ellicott City, MD 21042

December 30, 2022,

Performance: NAV: $7.08

Return: 17.32%

Investment Rank: 4%

FUND DETAILS:

Open to all investors

King Kovacs

Profile Style: Alternative

Long/Short Equity

Risk: average Minimum Investment Purchase: $1000

Maximum Front End Sales: no load

Net Expense Ratio: 1.15%

Inception Date: July 24, 2000

Number of Years of Gains: 12

Number of Years of Losses: 10

TOTAL NET ASSETS: $501.6 million

NET ASSET ALLOCATION:

U.S. Equity: 97.80%

Non–U.S. Equity: -24.18%

Fixed Income: 0%

Other: 0.78%

Cash: 25.60%

FIVE-YEAR RETURNS:

Year: 2022

Net Asset Value: $7.08   16.07%

Dividend Distribution: $08   1.25%

Total Return: 17.32%

2022 Best Mutual Funds

Year: 2021

Net Asset Value: $6.10 -0.65%

Dividend Distribution: $.03 0.42%

Total Return: -0.23%

Year: 2020

Net Asset Value: $6.14 14.34%

Dividend Distribution: $.01 0.19%

Total Return: 14.53%

Year: 2019

Net Asset Value: $5.37 -21.49%

Dividend Distribution: $.18 2.63%

Total Return: -18.86%

Year: 2018

Net Asset Value: $6.84 8.04%

Dividend Distribution: $.05 0.74%

Total Return: 8.78%

INVESTMENT RETURNS:

Year-to-date Return: 17.32%

average category: -5.35%

investment rank: 4%

3-year Return: 10.54%

average category: 4.28%

investment rank: 9%

5-year Return: 4.31%

average category: 3.61%

investment rank: 52%

10-year Return: -3.38%

average category: 5.01%

investment rank: 99%

3, 5, and 10-year Return annualized

$$$$$

Alternative Managed Futures

Investment Policy: The fund seeks to provide investment results that match the performance of a benchmark for measuring trends in the commodity and financial futures markets. The benchmark is constructed to capture both up and down price trends in physical commodities, global currencies, and US interest rate.

Arrow Managed Futures Strategy Fund A – MFTFX

877-277-6955

www.arrowfunds.com

Arrow Investment Trust

6100 Chevy Chase Dr

Laurel, DE 20707

December 30, 2022,

Performance: NAV: $6.69

Return: 57.65%

Investment Rank: 3%

King Kovacs

FUND DETAILS:

Open to all investors

Profile Style: Alternative Managed Futures

Risk: High

Minimum Investment Purchase: 5.75%

Maximum Front End Sales: no load

Net Expense Ratio: NA

Inception Date: April 29, 2010

Number of Years of Gains: 6

Number of Years of Losses: 6

TOTAL NET ASSETS: $31.40 million

NET ASSET ALLOCATION:

U.S. Equity: 0%

Fixed Income: 24.50%

Other: 61.04%

Cash: 14.27%

Non-Classified: 0.19%

FIVE-YEAR ANNUAL RETURNS:

Year: 2022

Net Asset Value: $6.69 10.95%

Dividend Distrib: $2.82 46.77%

Total Return: 57.65%

Year: 2021

Net Asset Value: $6.03 -0.17%

Dividend Distribution: $0.14 2.26%

Total Return: 2.09%

Year: 2020

Net Asset Value: $6.04 -4.13%

Dividend Distribution: $0.00

Total Return: -4.13%

Year: 2019

Net Asset Value: $6.30 -3.08%

Dividend Distribution: $1.19 18.30%

Total Return: 15.22%

Year: 2018

King Kovacs

Net Asset Value: $6.50 -25.37%

Dividend Distribution: $0.50 5.78%

Total Return: -19.59%

INVESTMENT RETURNS:

Year-to-date Return: 57.65%

average category: 14.85%

investment rank: 3%

3-year Return: 18.54%

average category: 8.19%

investment rank: 8%

5-year Return: 10.25%

average category: 4.18%

investment rank: 18%

10-year Return: 5.22%

average category: 3.98%

investment rank: 20%

3, 5, and 10-year Return annualized

$$$$$

Equity Income

Investment Policy: The fund seeks to provide current income as well as a long-term capital appreciation for its shareholders by investing at least 65% of its total assets in income-producing equity securities primarily.

Delaware Growth & Income Fund - FGINX

800-523-1918

Delaware Group Equity Funds IV
One Commerce Square, 2005 Market St
Philadelphia, PA 19103

December 30, 2022,
Performance: NAV: $13.57
Return: 3.09%
Investment Rank: 6%

FUND DETAILS:

Open to all investors
Profile Style: equity income
Risk: Average

King Kovacs

Minimum Investment Purchase: $1000

Maximum Front End Sales: 5.75%

Net Expense Ratio: 1.07%

Inception Date: October 4, 1993

Number of Years of Gains: 21

Number of Years of Losses: 8

TOTAL NET ASSETS: $1.02 billion

NET ASSET ALLOCATION:

U.S. Equity: 99.76%

Non-U.S. Equity: 0%

Fixed Income: 0%

Other: 0%

Cash: 0.24%

Non-Classified: 0%

FIVE-YEAR RETURNS:

Year: 2022

Net Asset Value: $13.57 -5.31%

Dividend Distribution: $1.19 8.40%

Total Return: 3.09%

2022 Best Mutual Funds

Year: 2021

Net Asset Value: $14.12 8.12%

Dividend Distribution: $1.75 13.38%

Total Return: 21.50%

Year: 2020

Net Asset Value: $13.06 -6.58%

Dividend Distribution: $0.91 6.50%

Total Return: -0.08%

Year: 2019

Net Asset Value: $13.98 –17.23%

Dividend Distribution: $7.16 42.38%

Total Return: 25.15%

Year: 2018

Net Asset Value: $16.89 -29.12%

Dividend Distribution: $4.45 18.67%

Total Return: -10.45%

INVESTMENT RETURNS:

King Kovacs

Year-to-date Return: 3.09%

average category: -7.41%

investment rank: 6%

3-year Return: 8.17%

average category: 6.68%

investment rank: 37%

5-year Return: 7.84%

average category: 6.98%

investment rank: 58%

10-year Return: 10.09%

average category: 10.03%

investment rank: 53%

3, 5, and 10-year Return annualized

$$$$$

2022 Best Mutual Funds

Equity Leverage

Investment Policy: The fund seeks daily investment results, before fees and expenses, that correspond to one and one-half times the return of the Dow Jones U.S. Oil & Gas Index for a single day, not for any other period. The Index seeks to measure the performance of particular companies in the oil and gas sector of the U.S. equity market.

Oil & Gas Ultra Pro Fund - ENPIX

800-776-3637

www.profunds.com

Profunds

3435 Stelzler Rd

Columbus, OH 43219

December 30, 2022,

Performance: NAV: $43.32

Return: 92.08%

Investment Rank: 3%

King Kovacs

FUND DETAILS:

Open to all investors

Profile Style: Equity Leverage

Risk: High

Minimum Investment Purchase $15,000

Maximum Front End Sales: no load

Net Expense Ratio: 1.78%

Inception Date: June 19, 2000

Number of Years of Gains: 14

Number of Years of Losses: 8

TOTAL NET ASSETS: $57.20 million

NET ASSET ALLOCATION:

U.S. Equity: 77.51%

Fixed Income: 0%

Other: 4.31%

Cash: 18.18%

Non-Classified: 0%

FIVE YEAR RETURNS

Year: 2022

2022 Best Mutual Funds

Net Asset Value: $43.32 86.80%

Dividend Distribution: $1.22 5.28%

Total Return: 92.08%

Year: 2021

Net Asset Value: $23.19 79.49%

Dividend Distribution: $0.37 2.86%

Total Return: 82.35%

Year: 2020

Net Asset Value: $12.92 -54.52%

Dividend Distribution: $0.23 0.79%

Total Return: -53.73%

Year: 2019

Net Asset Value: $28.41 6.28%

Dividend Distribution: $1.09 4.08%

Total Return: 10.36%

Year: 2018

Net Asset Value: $26.73 -30.06%

Dividend Distribution: $0.46 1.20%

King Kovacs

Total Return: -28.86%

INVESTMENT RETURNS:

Year-to-date Return: 92.08%

average category: -32.57%

investment rank: 3%

3-year Return: 40.23%

average category: -7.44%

investment rank: 1%

5-year Return: 20.44%

average category: -2.37%

investment rank: 37%

10-year Return: 2.21%

average category: 8.73%

investment rank: 77%

3, 5, and 10-year Return annualized

$$$$$

Financial Service

Investment Policy: The fund seeks capital appreciation. The fund invests at least 80% of the assets in the securities of companies principally engaged in underwriting, reinsuring, selling, distributing, or placing property and casualty, life, or health insurance, while using fundamental analysis of factors in selecting investment

Fidelity Select Insurance Portfolio - FSPCX

877-208-0098

www.fidelity.com

Fidelity Select Portfolios

82 Devonshire Street

Boston, MA 02109

December 30, 2022,

Performance:NAV: $74.05

Return: 7.76%

Investment Rank: 4%

FUND DETAILS:

Open to all investors

King Kovacs

Profile Style: Financial Services

Risk: below average

Minimum Investment Purchase: NA

Maximum Front End Sales: no load

Net Expense Ratio: 0.78%

Inception Date: December 16, 1985

Number of Years of Gains: 26

Number of Years of Losses: 11

TOTAL NET ASSETS: $301.90 million

NET ASSET ALLOCATION:

U.S. Equity: 88.30%

Non–U.S. Equity: 11.01%

Fixed Income: 0%

Other: 0%

Cash: 0.69%

FIVE-YEAR RETURNS:

Year: 2022

Net Asset Value: $74.05 6.95%

Dividend Distribution: $0.56 0.81%

2022 Best Mutual Funds

Total Return: 7.76%

Year: 2021

Net Asset Value: $69.24 18.43%

Dividend Distribution: $6.34 10.87%

Total Return: 29.30%

Year: 2020

Net Asset Value: $58.46 -9.60%

Dividend Distribution: $6.07 9.38%

Total Return: -0.22%

Year: 2019

Net Asset Value: $64.67 22.48%

Dividend Distribution: $3.99 7.55%

Total Return: 30.03%

Year: 2018

Net Asset Value: $52.80 -33.58%

Dividend Distribution: $17.76 22.34%

Total Return: -11.24%

INVESTMENT RETURNS:

Year-to-date Return: 7.76%%

average category: -15.43%%

investment rank: 4%

3-year Return: 12.28%

average category: 3.64%

investment rank: 5%

5-year Return: 11.13%

average category: 3.94%

 investment rank: 4%

10-year Return: 13.72%

average category: 9.44%

investment rank: 5%

3, 5, and 10-year Return annualized

$$$$$

Flexible Portfolio

Investment Policy: The fund seeks to generate a positive absolute return over time. Under normal market conditions, the fund seeks exposure to various asset classes, which may vary significantly over time but is generally expected to include exposure to equity markets, bond markets, interest rates, commodities, and currencies.

Guide Path Managed Futures Strategy Fund-GPMFX

888-278-5809

GPS Funds II

2300 Contra Costa Blvd., Suite 600

Pleasant Hill, DE 94523

December 30, 2022,

Performance: NAV: $9.06

Return: 36.33%

Investment rank: 1%

FUND DETAILS:

King Kovacs

Open to all investors

Profile Style: flexible portfolio

Risk: above average

Minimum Investment Purchase: NA

Maximum Front End Sales: no load

Net Expense Ratio: 1.54%

Inception Date: January 19, 2016

Number of Years of Gains: 5

Number of Years of Losses: 1

TOTAL NET ASSETS: $572.80 million

NET ASSET ALLOCATION:

U.S. Equity: 0%

Non–U.S. Equity: 0%

Fixed Income: 3.45%

Other: 6.17%

Cash: 90.38%

FIVE-YEAR RETURNS:

Year: 2022

Net Asset Value: $9.06 3.78%

2022 Best Mutual Funds

Dividend Distribution: $2.84 32.55%

Total Return: 36.33%

Year: 2021

Net Asset Value: $8.73 -1.58%

Dividend Distribution: $0.70 7.91%

Total Return: 6.33%

Year: 2020

Net Asset Value: $8.87 10.46%

Dividend Distribution: $0.30 3.72%

Total Return: 14.18%

Year: 2019

Net Asset Value: $8.03 3.35%

Dividend Distribution: $0.35 4.50%

Total Return: 7.85%

Year: 2018

Net Asset Value: $7.77 -13.22%

Dividend Distribution: $0.02 0.02%

Total Return: -13.20%

INVESTMENT RETURNS:

1-year Return: 36.33%

average category: -13.32%

investment rank: 1%

3-year Return: 18.95%

average category: 2.26%

investment rank: 2%

5-year Return: 10.30%

average category: 2.90%

investment rank: 2%

10-year Return:

average category: 5.08%

investment rank: --

3, 5, and 10-year Return annualized

$$$$$

Global Multi-Cap Value

Investment policy: The fund seeks long-term capital appreciation by investing principally in equity securities of companies in the gold and precious metals industries.

Vanguard Global Capital Cycles Fund-VGPMX

800-662-2739

www.vanguard.com

Vanguard Group

P.O. Box 2600 - V26

Valley Forge, PA 19482

December 30, 2022,

Performance: NAV: $11.50

Return: 7.39%

Investment Rank: 3%

King Kovacs

FUND DETAILS:

Open to all investors

Profile Style: Global

Risk: above average

Minimum Investment Purchase: $3000

Maximum Front End Sales: no load

Net Expense Ratio: 0.36%

Inception Date: May 23, 1984

Number of Years of Gains: 21

Number of Years of Losses: 17

TOTAL NET ASSETS: $1.26 billion

NET ASSET ALLOCATION:

U.S. Equity: 30.27%

Non–U.S. Equity: 58.64%

Fixed Income: 0%

Other: 0%

Cash: 11.10%

FIVE-YEAR ANNUAL RETURNS:

Year: 2022

Net Asset Value: $11.50 3.98%

Dividend Distribution: $0.38 3.41%

Total Return: 7.39%

Year: 2021

Net Asset Value: $11.06 15.69%

Dividend Distribution: $0.36 3.80%

Total Return: 19.49%

Year: 2020

Net Asset Value: $9.56 14.77%

Dividend Distribution: $0.20 2.44%

Total Return: 17.21%

Year: 2019

Net Asset Value: $8.33 18.66%

Dividend Distribution: $0.14 2.00%

Total Return: 20.66%

Year: 2018

King Kovacs

Net Asset Value: $7.02 -34.33%

Dividend Distribution: $0.22 2.06%

Total Return: -32.27%

INVESTMENT RETURNS:

1-year Return: 7.39%

average category: -22.51%

investment rank: 2%

3-year Return: 14.70%

average category: 3.67%

investment rank: 3%

5-year Return: 6.50%

average category: 4.30%

investment rank: 6%

10-year Return: 14.81%

average category: 8.43%

investment rank: 9%

3, 5, and 10-year Return annualized

$$$$$

Global Small-Cap Core

Investment Policy: The fund seeks long-term growth of capital by investing in U.S. and foreign equity stocks, including common stock, preferred stock, securities convertible into common stock, warrants, rights, and other equity securities having the characteristics of common stock (Such as depository receipts).

Kinetics Spin-Off/Corporation.Restructuring Fund-LSHAX

800-930-3828

www.kinectics.com

Kinetics Mutual Funds Inc

555 Taxter Road, Suite 175

Sleepy Hollow, NY 10591

December 30, 2022, Performance:

NAV: $25.05

Return: 39.45%

Investment Rank: 2%

King Kovacs

FUND DETAILS:

Open to all investors

Profile Style: Global

Risk: High

Minimum Investment Purchase: $2500

Maximum Front End Sales Load: 5.75%

Net Expense Ratio: 1.68%

Inception Date: May 4, 2007

Number of Years of Gains: 10

Number of Years of Losses: 5

TOTAL NET ASSETS: $10.10 million

NET ASSET ALLOCATION:

U.S. Equity: 89.31%

Non–U.S. Equity: 0%

Fixed Income: 0%

Other: 0%

Cash: 10.69%

FIVE-YEAR ANNUAL RETURNS:

Year: 2022

2022 Best Mutual Funds

Net Asset Value: $25.05 37.04%

Dividend Distribution: $0.44 2.41%

Total Return: 39.45%

Year: 2021

Net Asset Value: $18.28 42.59%

Dividend Distribution: $0.02 0.16%

Total Return: 42.75%

Year: 2020

Net Asset Value: $12.82 4.65%

Dividend Distribution: $0.07 0.56%

Total Return: 5.21%

Year: 2019

Net Asset Value: $12.25 32.00%

Dividend Distribution: $0.00

Total Return: 32.00%

Year: 2018

Net Asset Value: $9.28 -13.03%

Dividend Distribution: $0.50 4.73%

Total Return: -8.30%

INVESTMENT RETURNS:

1-year Return: 39.45%

average category: -22.57%

investment rank: 2%

3-year Return: 29.14%

average category: 3.67%

investment rank: 3%

5-year Return: 22.22%

average category: 4.30%

investment rank: 6%

10-year Return: 14.81%

average category: 8.43%

investment rank: 9%

3, 5, and 10-year Return annualized

$$$$$

2022 Best Mutual Funds

Health/Biotechnology

Investment Policy: The fund seeks long-term capital growth by primarily investing in common stocks of companies engaged in the research, development, production, or distribution of health-related products and services.

Live Oak Health Fund-LOGSX

888-462-5386

www.oakassociates.com

Oak Associates Funds

1 Freedom Valley Drive

Oaks, PA 19456

December 30, 2022, Performance:

NAV: $21.61

Return: 3.72%

Investment Rank: 1%

FUND DETAILS:

Open to all investors

King Kovacs

Profile Style: health/biotech

Risk: low

Minimum Investment Purchase: $2000

Maximum Front End Sales: no load

Net Expense Ratio: 1.00%

Inception Date: June 29, 2001

Number of Years of Gains: 16

Number of Years of Losses: 5

TOTAL NET ASSETS: $57.30 million

NET ASSET ALLOCATION:

U.S. Equity: 89.81%

Non–U.S. Equity: 3.24%

Fixed Income: 0%

Other: 0%

Cash: 6.95%

FIVE-YEAR ANNUAL RETURNS:

Year: 2022

Net Asset Value: $21.61 3.15%

Dividend Distribution: $.12 0.57%

Total Return: 3.72%

2022 Best Mutual Funds

Year: 202

Net Asset Value: $20.95 8.72%

Dividend Distribution: $1.69 8.79%

Total Return: 17.51%

Year: 2020

Net Asset Value: $19.27 1.00%

Dividend Distri $.95 4.98%

Total Return: 5.98%

Year: 2019

Net Asset Value: $19.08 18.00%

Dividend Distribution: $.16 0.98%

Total Return: 18.98%

Year: 2018

Net Asset Value: $16.17 -16.74%

Dividend Distribution: $2.48 12.79%

Total Return: -3.95%

INVESTMENT RETURNS:

1-year Return: 3.72%

average category: -13.31%

investment rank: 1%

3-year Return: 9.07%

average category: 5.74%

investment rank: 31%

5-year Return: 8.45%

average category: 7.49%

investment rank: 51%

10-year Return: 11.73%

average category: 13.17% 75%

investment rank: 13%

3, 5, and 10-year Return annualized

$$$$$

Large-Cap Value

Investment Policy: The fund seeks to provide long-term capital appreciation by investing in common stocks believed to be undervalued. Income is a secondary objective.

Hennessy Cornerstone Value Fund-HFCVX

800-966-4354

www.hennessyfunds.com

Hennessy Funds Trust

7250 Redwood Boulevard Suite 200

Novato, CA 94945

December 30, 2022, Performance:

NAV: $18.88

Return: 6.13%

Investment Rank: 1%

FUND DETAILS:

Open to all investors

Profile Style: growth and income

Risk: Average

Minimum Investment Purchase: $2500

Maximum Front End Sales Load: level

Net Expense Ratio: 1.23%

Inception Date: November 1, 1996

Number of Years of Gains: 21

Number of Years of Losses: 5

TOTAL NET ASSETS: $269.10 million

NET ASSET ALLOCATION:

U.S. Equity: 98.34%

Non–U.S. Equity: 0%

Fixed Income: 0%

Other: 0%

Cash: 1.66%

FIVE-YEAR ANNUAL RETURNS:

Year: 2022

Net Asset Value: $18.88 -3.77%

Dividend Distribution: $1.94 9.90%

Total Return: 6.13%

2022 Best Mutual Funds

Year: 2021

Net Asset Value: $19.62 23.86%

Dividend Distribution: $0.96 6.05%

Total Return: 29.91%

Year: 2020

Net Asset Value: $15.84 -8.76%

Dividend Distribution: $0.41 2.38%

Total Return: -6.38%

Year: 2019

Net Asset Value: $17.36 13.91%

Dividend Distribution: $1.05 6.88%

Total Return: 20.79%

Year: 2018

Net Asset Value: $15.24 -22.60%

Dividend Distribution: $2.61 13.26%

Total Return: -9.34%

INVESTMENT RETURNS:

1-year Return: 6.13%

average category: -6.90%

investment rank: 1%

3-year Return: 9.89%

average category: 7.02%

investment rank: 12%

5-year Return: 8.22%

average category: 7.32%

investment rank: 58%

10-year Return: 9.93%

average category: 10.57%

investment rank: 72%

3, 5, and 10-year Return annualized

$$$$$

Mid-Cap Core

Investment Policy: The fund seeks long-term capital growth by investing primarily in common stocks of companies with medium market capitalizations, which offer the potential for substantial long-term growth.

Janus Henderson Mid-Cap Value - JMCVX

877-335-2687

www.janushenderson.com

Janus Investment Fund

151 Detroit Street

Denver, CO 80206

December 31, 2021, Performance:

Net Asset Value: $14.89

Return: -5.10%

Investment Rank: 7%

FUND DETAILS:

Open to all investors

Profile Style: Growth

King Kovacs

Risk: below average

Minimum Investment Purchase: $2500

Maximum Front End Sales: no load

Net Expense Ratio: 0.74%

Inception Date: August 12, 1998

Number of Years of Gains: 18

Number of Years of Losses: 6

TOTAL NET ASSETS: $836.6 million

NET ASSET ALLOCATION:

U.S. Equity: 93.58%

Non–U.S. Equity: 4.18%

Fixed Income: 0%

Other: 0%

Cash: 2.24%

FIVE-YEAR ANNUAL RETURNS:

Year: 2022

Net Asset Value: $14.89 -10.78%

Dividend Distribution: $0.95 5.68%

Total Return: -5.10%

2022 Best Mutual Funds

Year: 2021

Net Asset Value: $16.69 6.04%

Dividend Distribution: $2.09 13.34%

Total Return: 19.38%

Year: 2020

Net Asset Value: $15.74 -2.48%

Dividend Distribution: $0.16 0.98%

Total Return: -1.50%

Year: 2019

Net Asset Value: $16.14 27.19%

Dividend Distribution: $0.38 2.97%

Total Return: 30.16%

Year: 2018

Net Asset Value: $12.69 -24.96%

Dividend Distribution: $1.97 11.64%

Total Return: -13.31%

INVESTMENT RETURNS:

King Kovacs

1-year Return: -5.10%

average category: -12.56%

investment rank: 7%

3-year Return: 4.26%

average category: 6.02%

investment rank: 84%

5-year Return: 5.93%

average category: 6.04%

investment rank: 75%

10-year Return: 8.59%

average category 9.86%

investment rank: 86%

3, 5, and 10-year Return annualized

$$$$$

Mid-Cap Growth

Investment Policy: The fund shapes long-term growth in value in the over-the-counter market. The fund will invest primarily in small companies that may grow faster than their larger competitors because of such factors as a new product, new technology, domination of a new market niche, or a more responsive management style.

Ave Maria Value Fund-AVEMX

888 726-9331

www.avemariafunds.com

Ave Maria Value Fund c/o Ultimus Fund Solutions, LLC

135 Merchant Street, Suite 230

Cincinnati, OH 45246

Year-to-Date: December 31, 2022

NAV: $24.05

Return: 4.18%

Investment Rank: 1%

FUND DETAILS:

Open to all investors

Profile Style: Growth

Risk: Average

Minimum Investment Purchase: $2500

Maximum Front End Sales: no load

Net Expense Ratio: 0.97%

Inception Date: May 1, 2001

Number of Years of Gains: 15

Number of Years of Losses: 6

TOTAL NET ASSETS: $340.56 million

NET ASSET ALLOCATION:

U.S. Equity: 87.81%

Non–U.S. Equity: 9.66%

Fixed Income: 0%

Other: 0%

Cash: 2.53%

FIVE-YEAR ANNUAL RETURNS:

Year: 2022

Net Asset Value: $24.05 3.00%

2022 Best Mutual Funds

Dividend Distribution: $0.28 1.18%

Total Return: 4.18%

Year: 2021

Net Asset Value: $23.35 15.77%

Dividend Distribution: $1.89 9.38%

Total Return: 25.15%

Year: 2020

Net Asset Value: $20.17 2.49%

Dividend Distribution: $0.72 3.67%

Total Return: 6.16%

Year: 2019

Net Asset Value: $19.68 14.49%

Dividend Distribution: $1.04 6.03%

Total Return: 20.52%

Year: 2018

Net Asset Value: $17.19 -17.67%

Dividend Distribution: $1.86 8.92%

Total Return: -8.75%

INVESTMENT RETURNS:

1-year Return: 4.18%

average category: -29.47%

investment rank: 1%

3-year Return: 11.83%

average category: 3.40%

investment rank: 2%

5-year Return: 9.45%

average category: 6.92%

investment rank: 20%

10-year Return: 8.54%

average category: 10.66%

investment rank: 89%

3, 5, and 10-year Return annualized

$$$$$

Mid-Cap Value

Investment policy: The fund seeks long-term growth of capital with income as a secondary consideration. The fund typically invests at least 80% of its assets in equity securities of U.S. companies with market capitalizations between $1 billion and $10 billion that are believed to have the potential for long-term capital growth.

Hotchkis & Wiley Mid-Cap Value A-HWMAX

866-493-8637
www.hwcm.com

Hotchkis & Wiley Funds

725 South Figueroa St., 39th Floor
Los Angeles, CA 90017-5439

December 30, 2022, Performance:

Net Asset Value: $44.03

Return: 1.42%

Investment rank: 6%

FUND DETAILS:

Open to all investors

King Kovacs

Profile Style: mid-cap

Risk: High

Minimum Investment Purchase: $2500

Maximum Front-End Sales: 5.25%

Net Expense Ratio: 1.21%

Inception Date: January 2, 2001

Number of Years of Gains: 15

Number of Years of Losses: 6

TOTAL NET ASSETS: $129.9 million

NET ASSET ALLOCATION:

U.S. Equity: 83.98%

Non–U.S. Equity: 12.84%

Fixed Income: 0%

Other: 0%

Cash: 3.18%

FIVE-YEAR ANNUAL RETURNS:

Year: 2022

Net Asset Value: $44.03 1.13%

Dividend Distribution: $0.13 0.29%

Total Return: 1.42%

2022 Best Mutual Funds

Year: 2021

Net Asset Value: $43.54 37.31%

Dividend Distribution: $0.52 1.63%

Total Return: 38.94%

Year: 2020

Net Asset Value: $31.71 1.95%

Dividend Distribution: $0.71 2.20%

Total Return: 4.15%

Year: 2019

Net Asset Value: $32.34 11.36%

Dividend Distribution: $0.39 1.33%

Total Return: 12.69%

Year: 2018

Net Asset Value: $29.04 -21.56%

Dividend Distribution: $0.76 2.05%

Total Return: -19.51%

INVESTMENT RETURNS:

1-year Return: 1.42%

average category: -6.65%

investment rank: 6%

3-year Return: 14.84%

average category: 7.05%

investment rank: 6%

5-year Return: 7.54%

average category: 5.65%

investment rank: 67%

10-year Return: 8.91%

average category: 9.30%

investment rank: 65%

3, 5, and 10-year Return annualized

$$$$$

Mixed-Asset: Target Allocation Growth

Investment Policy: The fund seeks high and dependable income consistent with proper growth. The fund invests at least 50% of its net assets in common or preferred stocks or securities convertible into common stock, which may or may not pay dividends.

Cantor FBP Appreciation & Income Opportunities Fund - FBPBX

866-738-1127
www.fbpfunds.com

Cantor FBP Appreciation & Income Opportunities Fund
C/O Ultimus Fund Solutions, LLC
225 Pictoria Drive, Suite 450
Cincinnati, OH 45246

December 30, 2022, Performance:

Net Asset Value: $19.98

Return: -4.59%

Investment Rank: 2%

FUND DETAILS:

Open to all investors

King Kovacs

Profile Style: balanced

Risk: above average

Minimum Investment Purchase: $5000

Maximum Front End Sales: no load

Net Expense Ratio: 1.05%

Inception Date: July 3, 1989

Number of Years of Gains: 26

Number of Years of Losses: 7

TOTAL NET ASSETS: $33.20 million

NET ASSET ALLOCATION:

U.S. Equity: 67.70%

Non–U.S. Equity: 1.95%

Fixed Income: 12.52%

Other: 0%

Cash: 17.83%

Non-Classified: 0%

FIVE-YEAR ANNUAL RETURNS:

Year: 2022

Net Asset Value: $19.98 -14.65%

2022 Best Mutual Funds

Dividend Distribution: $2.36 10.06%

Total Return: -4.59%

Year: 2021

Net Asset Value: $23.41 22.16%

Dividend Distribution: $1.16 6.03%

Total Return: 28.15%

Year: 2020

Net Asset Value: $19.17 0.42%

Dividend Distribution: $0.21 1.08%

Total Return: 1.50%

Year: 2019

Net Asset Value: $19.25 10.06%

Dividend Distribution: $1.27 7.24%

Total Return: 17.30%

Year: 2018

Net Asset Value: $17.49 -9.19%

Dividend Distribution: $0.67 3.47%

Total Return: -5.72%

INVESTMENT RETURNS:

1-year Return: -4.59%

average category: -15.30%

investment rank: 2%

3-year Return: 8.35%

average category: 3.30%

investment rank: 1%

5-year Return: 7.33%

average category: 4.46%

investment rank: 6%

10-year Return: 8.32%

average category: 7.06%

investment rank: 11%

3, 5, and 10-year Return annualized

$$$$$

Mixed-Asset: Target Allocation Moderate

Investment Policy: The fund seeks long-term capital growth, consistent with capital preservation and balanced by current income. The fund typically invests 50 to 60% of its assets in equity securities selected primarily for their growth potential and 40-50% in securities chosen primarily for their income potential.

Buffalo Flexible Income Fund - BUFBX

800-492-8332

www.buffalofunds.com

Buffalo funds

c/o U.S. Bank Global Fund Services

PO Box 701

Milwaukee, WI 53201-0701

December 31, 2022, Performance

Net Asset Value: $18.32

Return: 4.01%

Investment Rank: 1%

FUND DETAILS:

Open to all investors

Profile Style: balanced

Risk: below average

Minimum Investment Purchase: $2500

Maximum Front End Sales: no load

Net Expense Ratio: 1.01%

Inception Date: August 12, 1994

Number of Years of Gains: 22

Number of Years of Losses: 6

TOTAL NET ASSETS: $337 million

NET ASSET ALLOCATION:

U.S. Equity: 98.88%

Non–U.S. Equity: 0%

Fixed Income: 0%

Other: 0%

Cash: 1.12%

FIVE-YEAR ANNUAL RETURNS

Year: 2022

Net Asset Value: $18.32 -0.16%

Dividend Distribution: $0.77 4.17%

Total Return: 4.01%

Year: 2021

Net Asset Value: $18.35 22.66%

Dividend Distribution: $1.10 7.40%

Total Return: 30.00%

Year: 2020

Net Asset Value: $14.96 -5.56%

Dividend Distribution: $0.53 3.32%

Total Return: -2.24%

Year: 2019

Net Asset Value: $15.84 15.45%

Dividend Distribution: $0.45 3.31%

Total Return: 18.76%

Year: 2018

Net Asset Value: $13.72 -12.05%

King Kovacs

Dividend Distribution: $0.79 5.05%

Total Return: -7.00%

INVESTMENT RETURNS:

1-year Return: 4.01%

average category: -13.85%

investment rank: 1%

3-year Return: 10.59%

average category: 1.85%

investment rank: 1%

5-year Return: 8.71%

average category: 3.21%

investment rank: 1%

10-year Return: 8.05%

average category: 5.30%

investment rank: 4%

3, 5, and 10-year Return annualized

$$$$$

2022 Best Mutual Funds

Multi-Cap Core

Investment Policy: The fund seeks long-term growth of capital. The fund invests at least 80% of its net assets in equity securities of large capitalization U.S. companies with market capitalizations of less than $3.0 billion. The fund selects stocks that the Sub-Advisor believes yield a more accurate picture of a company's intrinsic value.

Center American Select Equity - DHAMX

855-298-4236
www. centrefunds.com/dhamx-dhanx

Centre Funds

48 Wall Street

New York, NY 10005

December 30, 2022, Performance:

NAV $13.39

Return: -3.31%

Investment Rank: 2%

FUND DETAILS:

Open to all investors

King Kovacs

Profile Style: growth

Risk: below average

Minimum Investment Purchase: $5000

Maximum Front End Sales: no load

Net Expense Ratio: 1.46%

Inception Date: December 21, 2011

Number of Years of Gains: 10

Number of Years of Losses: 1

TOTAL NET ASSETS: $269.9 million

NET ASSET ALLOCATION:

U.S. Equity: 97.31%

Non–U.S. Equity: 1.68%

Fixed Income: 0%

Other: 0%

Cash: 1.02%

Non-Classified: 0%

FIVE YEAR ANNUAL RETURNS:

Year: 2022

Net Asset Value: $13.39 -4.63%

2022 Best Mutual Funds

Dividend Distribution: $0.19 1.32%

Total Return: -3.31%

Year: 2021

Net Asset Value: $14.04 9.69%

Dividend Distribution: $2.27 17.70%

Total Return: 27.39%

Year: 2020

Net Asset Value: $12.80 25.12%

Dividend Distribution: $0.58 5.66%

Total Return: 30.78%

Year: 2019

Net Asset Value: $10.23 5.90%

Dividend Distribution: $1.02 10.54%

Total Return: 16.44%

Year: 2018

Net Asset Value: $9.66 -21.40%

Dividend Distribution: $2.18 17.75%

Total Return: -3.65%

INVESTMENT RETURNS:

1-year Return: -3.31%

average category: -18.04%

investment rank: 2%

3-year Return: 18.29%

average category: 5.94%

investment rank: 1%

5-year Return: 13.53%

average category: 7.19%

investment rank: 1%

10-year Return: 12.76%

average category: 10.67%

investment rank: 9%

3, 5, and 10-year Return annualized

$$$$$

Multi-Cap Growth

Investment Policy: The fund seeks long-term capital growth. The fund uses a quantitative investment process designed to identify common stocks of companies that currently have, or are expected to have, earnings and revenues that are not only growing but growing at an accelerating rate and that also have strong price momentum.

Schwartz Value Focused Fund - RCMFX

888-726-0753
www. schwartzinvest.com

Schwartz Value-Focused Fund

C/O Ultimus Fund Solutions, LLC

135 Merchant Street, Suite 230

Cincinnati, OH 45246

December 30, 2022, Performance

NAV: $45.06

Return: 21.15%

Investment Rank: 1%

King Kovacs

FUND DETAILS:

Open to all investors

Profile Style: growth

Risk: High

Minimum Investment Purchase: $2500

Maximum Front End Sales: no load

Net Expense Ratio: 1.25%

Inception Date: July 20, 1993

Number of Years of Gains: 29

Number of Years of Losses: 10

TOTAL NET ASSETS: $51.7 million

NET ASSET ALLOCATION:

U.S. Equity: 86.36%

Non–U.S. Equity: 6.77%

Fixed Income: 0%

Other: 0%

Cash: 6.87%

2022 Best Mutual Funds

FIVE-YEAR ANNUAL RETURNS:

Year: 2022

Net Asset Value: $45.06 20.10%

Dividend Distribution: $0.39 1.05%

Total Return: 21.15%

Year: 2021

Net Asset Value: $37.52 22.86%

Dividend Distribution: $2.53 8.28%

Total Return: 31.14%

Year: 2020

Net Asset Value: $30.54 8.95%

Dividend Distribution: $0.75 2.67%

Total Return: 11.62%

Year: 2019

Net Asset Value: $28.03 18.67%

Dividend Distribution: $0.00

Total Return: 18.67%

Year: 2018

Net Asset Value: $23.62 -10.67%

Dividend Distribution: $0.67 2.53%

Total Return: -8.14%

INVESTMENT RETURNS:

1-year Return: 21.15%

average category: -32.92%

investment rank: 1%

3-year Return: 21.30%

average category: 3.82%

investment rank: 2%

5-year Return: 14.89%

average category: 7.62%

investment rank: 3%

10-year Return: 10.22%

average category: 11.43%

investment rank: 76%

3, 5, and 10-year Return annualized

$$$$$

Multi-Cap Value

Investment Policy: The Fund seeks to provide capital growth and preservation by investing primarily in common stock. The Fund seeks to provide above-average performance in both rising and falling market periods by investing in stocks that have limited downside risk with positive upside potential.

Muhlenkamp Fund - MUHLX
800-860-3863
www.muhlenkamp.com

Managed Portfolio Series
615 East Michigan Street
Milwaukee, WI 53202

December 30, 2022, Performance:
NAV: $55.11
Return: 2.88%

Investment Rank: 1%

King Kovacs

FUND DETAILS:

Open to all investors

Profile Style: growth

Risk: average

Minimum Investment Purchase: $1500

Maximum Front End Sales: No load

Net Expense Ratio: 1.10%

Inception Date: November 1, 1988

Number of Years of Gains: 25

Number of Years of Losses: 9

TOTAL NET ASSETS: $293.50 million

NET ASSET ALLOCATION:

U.S. Equity: 52.80%

Non–U.S. Equity: 0%

Fixed Income: 0%

Other: 0%

Cash: 47.20%

Non-Classified: 0%

2022 Best Mutual Funds

FIVE YEAR ANNUAL RETURNS:

Year: 2022
 Net Asset Value: $55.11 -3.67%
Dividend Distribution: $3.75 6.55%
Total Return: 2.88%

Year: 2021
Net Asset Value: $57.21 19.71%
Dividend Distribution: $4.45 9.31%
Total Return: 29.02%

Year: 2020
Net Asset Value: $47.79 1.42%
Dividend Distribution:$4.87 10.34%
Total Return: 11.86%

Year: 2019
Net Asset Value: $47.12 12.97%
Dividend Distribution: $0.59 1.42%
Total Return: 14.39%

Year: 2018
Net Asset Value: $41.71 -24.45%
Dividend Distribution:$6.16 11.16%

Total Return: -13.29%

INVESTMENT RETURNS:
1-year Return: 2.88%
average category: -6.75%
investment rank: 1%

3-year Return: 14.59%
average category: 6.99%
investment rank: 1%

5-year Return: 8.97%
average category: 6.70%
investment rank: 21%

10-year Return: 8.08%
average category: 10.16%
investment rank: 93%
3, 5, and 10-year Return annualized

$$$$$

Sector: Natural Resources

Investment Policy: The Fund seeks capital appreciation. The Fund normally invests at least 80% of assets in securities of companies principally engaged in the energy field, including the conventional areas of oil, gas, electricity, and coal, and newer sources of energy such as nuclear, geothermal, oil shale, and solar power.

Fidelity Select Energy Portfolio-FSENX
877-208-0098

www.fidelity.com

Fidelity Investments

P.O. Box 5000

Cincinnati, OH 45273-8610

December 30, 2022, Performance:

NAV $56.11

Return: 63.03%

Investment Rank: 8% hmm

FUND DETAILS:

Open to all investors

Profile Style: Natural resource

Risk: average

Minimum Investment Purchase: NA

Maximum Front End Sales: no load

Net Expense Ratio: 0.77%

Inception Date: July 14, 1981

Number of Years of Gains: NA

Number of Years of Losses: NA

TOTAL NET ASSETS: $3.22 billion

NET ASSET ALLOCATION:

U.S. Equity: 89.76%

Non–U.S. Equity: 9.99%

Fixed Income: 0%

Other: 0%

Cash: 0.25%

Non-Classified: 0%

FIVE YEAR ANNUAL RETURNS:

Year: 2022

2022 Best Mutual Funds

Net Asset Value: $56.11 58.86%

Dividend Distribution: $1.47 4.17%

Total Return: 63.03%

Year: 2021

Net Asset Value: $35.32 38.83%

Dividend Distribution: $3.85 16.52%

Total Return: 55.35%

Year: 2020

Net Asset Value: $23.28 -34.81%

Dividend Distribution: $0.82 2.30%

Total Return: -32.51%

Year: 2019

Net Asset Value: $35.71 7.89%

Dividend Distribution: $0.66 1.78%

Total Return: 9.88%

Year: 2018

Net Asset Value: $33.10 -25.93%

Dividend Distribution: $0.45 1.01%

Total Return: -24.92%

INVESTMENT RETURNS:
1-year Return: 63.03%
average category: 46.06%
investment rank: 8%

3-year Return:
average category: 14.96%
investment rank: 22%

5-year Return:
average category: 2.92%
investment rank: 27%

10-year Return: 4.94%
average category: 0.37%
investment rank: 22%
3, 5, and 10-year Return annualized

$$$$$

2022 Best Mutual Funds

Small-Cap Core

Investment Policy: The Fund seeks long-term, tax-efficient capital appreciation with limited downsiderisk through investing primarily in equitysecurities of smaller growth companies which the Fund believes are trading at a discount.

Auer Growth Fund - AUERX

888-711-2837

www.sbauerfunds.com

Auer Growth Fund
Unified Series Trust
2960 N. Meridian Street, Suite 300
Indianapolis, IN 46208

December 30, 2022, Performance:
NAV: $12.80
Return: 9.97%
Investment Rank: 1%

FUND DETAILS:

Open to all investors

King Kovacs

Profile Style: small cap

Risk: above average

Minimum Investment Purchase: $2000

Maximum Front End Sales: no load

Net Expense Ratio: 2.37%

Inception Date: December 28, 2007

Number of Years of Gains: 9

Number of Years of Losses: 6

TOTAL NET ASSETS: $37.70 million

NET ASSET ALLOCATION:

U.S. Equity: 93.45%

Non–U.S. Equity: 4.49%

Fixed Income: 0%

Other: 0%

Cash: 2.06%

Non-Classified: 0%

FIVE YEAR ANNUAL RETURNS:

Year: 2022

Net Asset Value: $12.80   3.90%

Dividend Distribution: $.75   6.07%

Total Return: 9.97%

2022 Best Mutual Funds

Year: 2021
Net Asset Value: $12.32   45.11%
Dividend Distribution: $0.00
Total Return: 45.11%

Year: 2020
Net Asset Value: $8.49   -1.85%
Dividend Distribution: $0.00
Total Return: -1.85%

Year: 2019
Net Asset Value: $8.65 27.96%
Dividend Distribution: $0.00
Total Return: 27.96%

Year: 2018
Net Asset Value: 6.76% -25.63%
Dividend Distribution: $0.00
Total Return: -25.63%

INVESTMENT RETURNS:

1-year Return: 9.97%
average category: -14.43%
investment rank: 1%

3-year Return: 17.74%
average category: 5.34%
investment rank: 1%

5-year Return: 11.11%
average category: 4.70%
investment rank: 3%

10-year Return: 8.83%
average category: 9.08%
investment rank: 60%
3, 5, and 10-year Return annualized

$$$$$

2022 Best Mutual Funds

Small-Cap Growth

Investment Policy: The Fund seeks long-term capital growth through investments in a diversified portfolio of common stocks the Fund Advisor believes to possess superior growth potential.

Kinetics Paradigm Fund - WWNPX

800-930-3828

www.kineticsfunds.com

Kinetics Mutual Funds Inc
555 Taxter Road, Suite 175
Sleepy Hollow, NY 10591

December 30, 2022
NAV: $92.91
Return: 29.18%
Investment rank: 1%

FUND DETAILS:

Open to all investors

King Kovacs

Profile Style: small cap

Risk: high

Minimum Investment Purchase: $2500

Maximum Front End Sales: no load

Net Expense Ratio: 1.64%

Inception Date: December 31, 1999

Number of Years of Gains: 17

Number of Years of Losses: 6

TOTAL NET ASSETS: $489.60 million

NET ASSET ALLOCATION:

U.S. Equity: 90.14%

Non–U.S. Equity: 0%

Fixed Income: 0%

Other: 0%

Cash: 9.86%

Non-Classified: 0%

FIVE YEAR ANNUAL RETURNS:

Year: 2022

Net Asset Value: $92.91   26.63%

Dividend Distribution: $1.87   2.55%

2022 Best Mutual Funds

Total Return: 29.18%

Year: 2021
Net Asset Value: $73.37 35.90%
Dividend Distribution: $1.21 2.25%
Total Return: 38.15%

Year: 2020
Net Asset Value: $53.99 1.14%
Dividend Distribution: $1.16 2.18%
Total Return: 3.32%

Year: 2019
Net Asset Value: $53.38 29.19%
Dividend Distribution: $0.53 1.29%
Total Return: 30.48%

Year: 2018
Net Asset Value: $41.32 -14.49%
Dividend Distribution: $4.32 8.94%
Total Return: -5.55%

INVESTMENT RETURNS:
1-year Return: 29.18%
average category: -26.65%

King Kovacs

investment rank: 1%

3-year Return: 23.55%
average category: 3.61%
investment rank: 1%

5-year Return: 19.12%
average category: 6.14%
investment rank: 1%

10-year Return: 16.68%
average category: 10.17%
investment rank: 1%
3, 5, and 10-year Return annualized

$$$$$

Small-Cap Value

Investment Policy: The Fund seeks to provide long-term total Return of capital, primarily through capital appreciation. The Fund invest in a diversified portfolio of small stocks. Bridgeway Funds define small stocks as companies that are smaller than the largest 500 U.S. companies as measured by market capitalization.

Invesco Small-Cap Value Fund- VSCAX

800-959-4246

www.invesco.com

Aim Sector Funds
11 Greenway Plaza, Suite 100
Houston, TX 77046

December 30, 2022, Performance:
NAV: $17.36
Return: 4.32%
Investment Rank: 3%

FUND DETAILS:

Open to all investors
Profile Style: small cap

King Kovacs

Risk: high

Minimum Investment Purchase: $1000

Maximum Front-End Sales: 5.50%

Net Expense Ratio: 1.09%

Inception Date: June 21, 1999

Number of Years of Gains: 17

Number of Years of Losses: 6

TOTAL NET ASSETS: $2.6 billion

NET ASSET ALLOCATION:

U.S. Equity: 80.90%

Non–U.S. Equity: 14.62%

Fixed Income: 0%

Other: 0%

Cash: 4.49%

Non-Classified: 0%

FIVE-YEAR ANNUAL RETURNS:

Year: 2022

Net Asset Value: $17.36   -5.45%

Dividend Distribution: $1.79   9.77%

Total Return: 4.32%

Year: 2021

2022 Best Mutual Funds

Net Asset Value $18.36 15.98%

Dividend Distrib: $3.25 20.53%

Total Return: 36.51%

Year: 2020

Net Asset Value: $15.83 10.47%

Dividend Distribution: $0.05 0.34%

Total Return: 10.81%

Year: 2019

Net Asset Value: $14.33 21.13%

Dividend Distrib: $1.29 10.92%

Total Return: 32.05%

Year: 2018

Net Asset Value: $11.83 -35.28%

Dividend Distribution: $1.83 9.99%

Total Return: -25.29%

INVESTMENT RETURNS:

1-year Return: 4.32

average category: -8.56%

investment rank: 3%

3-year return: 17.21%
average category: 7.84%
investment rank: 4%

5-year return: 11.70%
average category: 4.82%
investment rank: 5%

10-year return: 12.16%
average category: 8.78%
investment rank: 3%
3, 5, and 10 returns are Annualized

$$$$$

Utility

Investment Policy: The Fund seeks investment income and capital appreciation results that correlate to the performance of an index comprising the common stocks of natural gas distribution and transmission company members of the American Gas Association.

Hennessy Gas Utility Fund-GASFX

800-966-4354

www.hennessyfunds.com

Hennessy Funds Trust

7250 Redwood Boulevard Suite 200

Novato, CA 94945

December 30, 2022, Performance

NAV: $24.56

Return: 6.15%

Investment Rank: 4%

FUND DETAILS:

Open to all investors

King Kovacs

Profile Style: utility

Risk: average

Minimum Investment Purchase: $2500

Maximum Front-End Sales: level

Net Expense Ratio: 1.00%

Inception Date: May 10, 1989

Number of Years of Gains: 24

Number of Years of Losses: 9

TOTAL NET ASSETS: $484.1 million

NET ASSET ALLOCATION:

U.S. Equity: 99.34%

Non–U.S. Equity: 0%

Fixed Income: 0%

Other: 0%

Cash: 0.66%

Non-Classified: 0%

FIVE YEAR ANNUAL RETURNS:

Year: 2022

Net Asset Value: $24.56 -2.35%

Dividend Distrib: $2.14 8.50%

Total Return: 6.15%

2022 Best Mutual Funds

Year: 2021

Net Asset Value: $25.15 7.62%

Dividend Distribution $2.78 11.90%

Total Return: 19.52%

Year: 2020

Net Asset Value: $23.37 -18.32%

Dividend Distribution $2.57 9.00%

Total Return: -9.32%

Year: 2019

Net Asset Value: $28.61 12.46%

Dividend Distribution: $2.12 8.32%

Total Return: 20.78%

Year: 2018

Net Asset Value: $25.44 -13.62%

Dividend Distribution $2.98 10.11%

Total Return: -3.51%

INVESTMENT RETURNS:

1-year Return: 6.15%

average category: -0.35%

investment rank: 4%

3-year Return: 5.45%

average category: 5.39%
investment rank: 49%

5-year Return: 6.72%
average category: 7.99%
investment rank: 85%

10-year Return: 8.43%
average category: 9.34%
investment rank: 76%
3, 5, and 10-year Return annualized

$$$$$

Multi-Cap Value

Investment Policy: The Fund seeks capital growth and preservation by investing primarily in common stock. The Fund seeks to provide above-average performance in both rising and falling market periods by investing in stocks that have limited downside risk with positive upside potential.

Muhlenkamp Fund-MUHLX

800-860-3863

www.muhlenkamp.com

Managed Portfolio Series

615 East Michigan Street

Milwaukee, WI 53202

December 30, 2022, Performance:

NAV: $55.11

 return: 2.88%

Investment Rank: 1%

FUND DETAILS:

Open to all investors

Profile Style: growth

Risk: average

Minimum Investment Purchase: $1500

Maximum Front-End Sales: No load

Net Expense Ratio: 1.10%

Inception Date: November 1, 1988

Number of Years of Gains: 25

Number of Years of Losses: 9

TOTAL NET ASSETS: $293.50 million

NET ASSET ALLOCATION:

U.S. Equity: 52.80%

Non–U.S. Equity: 0%

Fixed Income: 0%

Other: 0%

Cash: 47.20%

Non-Classified: 0%

FIVE-YEAR ANNUAL RETURNS:

Year: 2022

Net Asset Value: $55.11 -3.67%

Dividend Distribution: $3.75 6.55%

Total return: 2.88%

Year: 2021

Net Asset Value: $57.21 19.71%

Dividend Distribution: $4.45 9.31%

Total return: 29.02%

Year: 2020

Net Asset Value: $47.79 1.42%

Dividend Distribution:$4.87 10.34%

Total return: 11.86%

Year: 2019

Net Asset Value: $47.12 12.97%

Dividend Distribution: $0.59 1.42%

Total return: 14.39%

Year: 2018

Net Asset Value: $41.71 -24.45%

Dividend Distribution:$6.16 11.16%

Total return: -13.29%

INVESTMENT RETURNS:

1-year return: 2.88%

average category: -6.75%

investment rank: 1%

3-year return: 14.59%

average category: 6.99%

investment rank: 1%

2022 Best Mutual Funds

5-year return: 8.97%

average category: 6.70%

investment rank: 21%

10-year return: 8.08%

average category: 10.16%

investment rank: 93%

3, 5, and 10-year return annualized

$$$$$

Sector: Natural Resources

Investment Policy: The Fund seeks capital appreciation. The Fund normally invests at least 80% of assets in securities of companies principally engaged in the energy field, including the conventional areas of oil, gas, electricity, and coal, and newer energy sources such as nuclear, geothermal, oil shale, and solar power.

Fidelity Select Energy Portfolio-FSENX

877-208-0098

www.fidelity.com

Fidelity Investments

P.O. Box 5000

Cincinnati, OH 45273-8610

December 30, 2022, Performance:

NAV $56.11

return: 63.03%

Investment Rank: 8% hmm

FUND DETAILS:

Open to all investors

Profile Style: Natural resource

Risk: average

Minimum Investment Purchase: NA

Maximum Front End Sales: no load

Net Expense Ratio: 0.77%

Inception Date: July 14, 1981

Number of Years of Gains: NA

Number of Years of Losses: NA

TOTAL NET ASSETS: $3.22 billion

NET ASSET ALLOCATION:

U.S. Equity: 89.76%

Non–U.S. Equity: 9.99%

Fixed Income: 0%

Other: 0%

Cash: 0.25%

Non-Classified: 0%

FIVE-YEAR ANNUAL RETURNS:

Year: 2022

Net Asset Value: $56.11 58.86%

Dividend Distribution: $1.47 4.17%

Total return: 63.03%

Year: 2021

Net Asset Value: $35.32 38.83%

Dividend Distribution:$3.85 16.52%

Total return: 55.35%

Year: 2020

Net Asset Value: $23.28 -34.81%

Dividend Distribution: $0.82 2.30%

Total return: -32.51%

Year: 2019

2022 Best Mutual Funds

Net Asset Value: $35.71 7.89%

Dividend Distribution: $0.66 1.78%

Total return: 9.88%

Year: 2018

Net Asset Value: $33.10 -25.93%

Dividend Distribution: $0.45 1.01%

Total return: -24.92%

INVESTMENT RETURNS:

1-year return: 63.03%

average category: 46.06%

investment rank: 8%

3-year return:

average category: 14.96%

investment rank: 22%

5-year return:

average category: 2.92%

investment rank: 27%

10-year return: 4.94%

average category: 0.37%

investment rank: 22%

3, 5, and 10-year return annualized

$$$$$

Small-Cap Core

Investment Policy: The Fund seeks long-term, tax-efficient capital appreciation with limited downside risk through investing primarily in equity securities of smaller growth companies that the Fund believes are trading at a discount.

Auer Growth Fund - AUERX

888-711-2837

www.sbauerfunds.com

Auer Growth Fund

Unified Series Trust

2960 N. Meridian Street, Suite 300

Indianapolis, Indiana 46208

December 30, 2022, Performance:

NAV: $12.80

return: 9.97%

Investment Rank: 1%

FUND DETAILS:

Open to all investors

Profile Style: small cap

Risk: above average

Minimum Investment Purchase: $2000

Maximum Front End Sales: no load

Net Expense Ratio: 2.37%

Inception Date: December 28, 2007

Number of Years of Gains: 9

Number of Years of Losses: 6

TOTAL NET ASSETS: $37.70 million

NET ASSET ALLOCATION:

U.S. Equity: 93.45%

Non–U.S. Equity: 4.49%

Fixed Income: 0%

Other: 0%

Cash: 2.06%

Non-Classified: 0%

FIVE-YEAR ANNUAL RETURNS:

Year: 2022

Net Asset Value: $12.80 3.90%

Dividend Distribution: $.75 6.07%

Total return: 9.97%

Year: 2021

Net Asset Value: $12.32 45.11%

Dividend Distribution: $0.00

Total return: 45.11%

Year: 2020

Net Asset Value: $8.49 -1.85%

Dividend Distribution: $0.00

Total return: -1.85%

Year: 2019

Net Asset Value: $8.65 27.96%

Dividend Distribution: $0.00

Total return: 27.96%

Year: 2018

Net Asset Value: 6.76% -25.63%

Dividend Distribution: $0.00

Total return: -25.63%

INVESTMENT RETURNS:

1-year return: 9.97%

average category: -14.43%

investment rank: 1%

3-year return: 17.74%

average category: 5.34%

investment rank: 1%

2022 Best Mutual Funds

5-year return: 11.11%

average category: 4.70%

investment rank: 3%

10-year return: 8.83%

average category: 9.08%

investment rank: 60%

3, 5, and 10-year return annualized

$$$$$

Small-Cap Growth

Investment Policy: The Fund seeks long-term growth of capital through investments in a diversified portfolio of common stocks believed by the Fund Advisor to possess superior growth potential.

Kinetics Paradigm Fund-WWNPX

800-930-3828

www.kineticsfunds.com

Kinetics Mutual Funds Inc

555 Taxter Road, Suite 175

Sleepy Hollow NY 10591

December 30, 2022

NAV: $92.91

return: 29.18%

Investment rank: 1%

FUND DETAILS:

Open to all investors

Profile Style: small cap

Risk: high

Minimum Investment Purchase: $2500

Maximum Front End Sales: no load

Net Expense Ratio: 1.64%

Inception Date: December 31, 1999

Number of Years of Gains: 17

Number of Years of Losses: 6

TOTAL NET ASSETS: $489.60 million

NET ASSET ALLOCATION:

U.S. Equity: 90.14%

Non–U.S. Equity: 0%

Fixed Income: 0%

Other: 0%

Cash: 9.86%

Non-Classified: 0%

FIVE-YEAR ANNUAL RETURNS:

Year: 2022

Net Asset Value: $92.91 26.63%

Dividend Distribution: $1.87 2.55%

Total return: 29.18%

Year: 2021

Net Asset Value: $73.37 35.90%

Dividend Distribution: $1.21 2.25%

Total return: 38.15%

Year: 2020

Net Asset Value: $53.99 1.14%

Dividend Distribution: $1.16 2.18%

Total return: 3.32%

2022 Best Mutual Funds

Year: 2019

Net Asset Value: $53.38 29.19%

Dividend Distribution: $0.53 1.29%

Total return: 30.48%

Year: 2018

Net Asset Value: $41.32 -14.49%

Dividend Distribution: $4.32 8.94%

Total return: -5.55%

INVESTMENT RETURNS:

1-year return: 29.18%

average category: -26.65%

investment rank: 1%

3-year return: 23.55%

average category: 3.61%

investment rank: 1%

5-year return: 19.12%

average category: 6.14%

investment rank: 1%

10-year return: 16.68%

average category: 10.17%

investment rank: 1%

3, 5, and 10-year return annualized

$$$$$

2022 Best Mutual Funds

Small-Cap Value

Investment Policy: The Fund seeks to provide a long-term total return of capital, primarily through capital appreciation. The Fund invests in a diversified portfolio of small stocks. Bridgeway Funds define small stocks as companies that are smaller than the largest 500 U.S. companies as measured by market capitalization.

Invesco Small-Cap Value Fund VSCAX

800-959-4246

www.invesco.com

Aim Sector Funds

11 Greenway Plaza, Suite 100

Houston, TX 77046

December 30, 2022, Performance:

NAV: $17.36

return: 4.32%

Investment Rank #3

King Kovacs

FUND DETAILS:

Open to all investors

Profile Style: small cap

Risk: high

Minimum Investment Purchase: $1000

Maximum Front End Sales: 5.50%

Net Expense Ratio: 1.09%

Inception Date: June 21, 1999

Number of Years of Gains: 17

Number of Years of Losses: 6

TOTAL NET ASSETS: $2.6 billion

NET ASSET ALLOCATION:

U.S. Equity: 80.90%

Non–U.S. Equity: 14.62%

Fixed Income: 0%

Other: 0%

Cash: 4.49%

Non-Classified: 0%

FIVE-YEAR ANNUAL RETURNS:

Year: 2022

Net Asset Value: $17.36 -5.45%

Dividend Distribution: $1.79 9.77%

Total return: 4.32%

Year: 2021

Net Asset Value $18.36 15.98%

Dividend Distrib: $3.25 20.53%

Total return: 36.51%

Year: 2020

Net Asset Value: $15.83 10.47%

Dividend Distribution: $0.05 0.34%

Total return: 10.81%

Year: 2019

Net Asset Value: $14.33 21.13%

Dividend Distrib: $1.29 10.92%

Total return: 32.05%

Year: 2018

Net Asset Value: $11.83 -35.28%

Dividend Distribution: $1.83 9.99%

Total return: -25.29%

INVESTMENT RETURNS:

1-year return: 4.32

average category: -8.56%

investment rank: 3%

3-year return: 17.21%

average category: 7.84%

investment rank: 4%

2022 Best Mutual Funds

5-year return: 11.70%

average category: 4.82%

investment rank: 5%

10-year return: 12.16%

average category: 8.78%

investment rank: 3%

3, 5, and 10 returns are Annualized

$$$$$

Utility

Investment Policy: The Fund seeks investment income and capital appreciation results that correlate to the performance of an index comprising the common stocks of natural gas distribution and transmission company members of the American Gas Association.

Hennessy Gas Utility Fund-GASFX

800-966-4354

www.hennessyfunds.com

Hennessy Funds Trust

7250 Redwood Boulevard Suite 200

Novato CA 94945

December 30, 2022, Performance

NAV: $24.56

 return: 6.15%

Investment Rank: 4%

FUND DETAILS:

Open to all investors

Profile Style: Utility

Risk: Average

Minimum Investment Purchase: $2500

Maximum Front-End Sales: Level

Net Expense Ratio: 1.00%

Inception Date: May 10, 1989

Number of Years of Gains: 24

Number of Years of Losses: 9

TOTAL NET ASSETS: $484.1 million

NET ASSET ALLOCATION:

U.S. Equity: 99.34%

Non–U.S. Equity: 0%

Fixed Income: 0%

Other: 0%

Cash: 0.66%

Non-Classified: 0%

FIVE-YEAR ANNUAL RETURNS:

Year: 2022

Net Asset Value: $24.56 -2.35%

Dividend Distrib: $2.14 8.50%

Total return: 6.15%

Year: 2021

Net Asset Value: $25.15 7.62%

Dividend Distribution $2.78 11.90%

Total return: 19.52%

Year: 2020

Net Asset Value: $23.37 -18.32%

Dividend Distribution $2.57 9.00%

Total return: -9.32%

2022 Best Mutual Funds

Year: 2019

Net Asset Value: $28.61 12.46%

Dividend Distribution: $2.12 8.32%

Total return: 20.78%

Year: 2018

Net Asset Value: $25.44 -13.62%

Dividend Distribution $2.98 10.11%

Total return: -3.51%

INVESTMENT RETURNS:

1-year return: 6.15%

average category: -0.35%

investment rank: 4%

3-year return: 5.45%

average category: 5.39%

investment rank: 49%

5-year return: 6.72%

average category: 7.99%

investment rank: 85%

10-year return: 8.43%

average category: 9.34%

investment rank: 76%

3, 5, and 10-year return annualized

$$$$$

Self-Directed Retirement Investing

If you are a wage earner and middle-aged or older, invest in one of the best types of investment portfolios to build a nest egg (IRA). Time waits for no one. Every year each of us is a little older. It is essential to plan and be prepared for retirement today, not tomorrow. This can best be achieved by establishing a goal, committing to the goal, and persevering.

Establishing Goal: You, the investor of a mutual fund, must determine which goal in your investment would best achieve the financial return for you:

Aggressive goals are methods to achieve maximum returns. An aggressive investment strategy attempts to grow assets above average compared to its industry or the overall market.

Conservative goals are investment strategies that grow capital over the long term. This minimizes the risk by investing in companies that show growth over time. Conservative growth mutual funds have minimal asset turnover or a high percentage of fixed assets and use a buy-hold investment strategy.

Moderate goals are investments that attempt to reduce risks and increase returns equally. The investment may incur a short-term loss of principal. And the lower degree of liquidity in exchange for long-term appreciation.

Perseverance: It is difficult to save money, especially when encountering hard times. You, the investor, must save as much money as possible, even under those conditions. Once the crisis no longer exists, continue investing as planned.

Commitment: To succeed in your endeavor, you must commit to the money saved and invested in your retirement portfolio. After making the minimum investment, you can make weekly, bi-weekly, every month or annual investment payments. You cannot exceed the maximum investment for the IRA year.

Each year the maximum investment you can contribute to your traditional IRA and Roth IRA is $5500 for individuals under the age of 50. The maximum investment is $6500 for individuals who are 50 years of age or older.

Individual Retirement Account

An individual Retirement Account (IRA) is one of the best investments available when planning for retirement. As an owner of IRA accounts, you make all the decisions on the investment's success or failure. You manage and control the assets in the investment. You decide if the investment will be aggressive, moderate, or conservative. You determine how much money will be invested and how often.

Traditional IRAs are a great way to save for the future! All reinvested mutual fund income and capital gains distribution is not taxable until you reach the age of 72.

Internal Revenue Service guidelines:

https://www.irs.gov/retirement-plans/traditional-and-roth-iras

Contribution Limits: In 2022, the maximum that can be contributed to all Traditional and Roth IRAs is $6,000 under 50 years of age, or the maximum is $7,000 when older.

IRS Withholding Calculator: This helps to determine federal income tax withholding so your employer can withhold the correct amount from your salary. This is especially helpful if you are starting a new job.

IRA Contribution at age 72: You cannot make contributions

to traditional IRA investments. However, you can still contribute to a Roth IRA and make rollover contributions to a Roth IRA.

Roth IRA contribution limit: The same general contribution applies to both Roth and traditional IRAs.

Required Minimum Distribution RMD: the IRS requires that you take the mutual fund distribution once you reach the age of 72. You may be subject to a 50% non-deductible federal excise tax

Tax Exempt: Investment income or capital gain distributions that are reinvested are tax exempt until reaching 72.

The Investor Government required minimum distribution calculator determines the total dollar amount that must be taken for the year.

www.investor.gov/financial-tools-calculators/required-minimum-distribution-calculator

Investors do not have to withdraw money from only one specific IRA Investment. Withdrawals can be from several portfolio IRA investments.

Make sure that the total Required Minimum Distribution withdrawals are correct for the current year. The RMD money withdrawals can be used for:

Reinvestment in the mutual fund:

This is an excellent choice because reinvesting in the mutual fund provides additional shares of an investment, and you purchase these shares on the dollar-cost-average.

Rollover of IRA investments:

Limited to making only one rollover each year. If you make a rollover, you must roll over the money withdrawn from one investment into another investment within 60 days from date of withdrawal.

Retirement Planning:

Select mutual fund investments that provide consistent above-average performance. Investors should make mutual fund investments ranked at the top of the investment category. Be sure that most years of performance have more return gains and fewer return losses.

Decide which type of risk, low-risk, moderate-risk, or high-risk, will best achieve the retirement nest egg goal.

Remember, you can choose IRA asset allocation for your retirement portfolio. Will you choose mutual funds, certificates of deposit, annuities, or a combination for your retirement portfolio?

King Kovacs

Mutual Fund Investing

Here is a narrative describing the essence of a mutual fund and the important investment terms you should understand and be familiar with when making investments.

In the United States, a mutual fund is an investment regulated by the Securities & Exchange Commission. Most mutual funds are listed on the NASDAQ market.

Mutual funds collect investments from investors and pool the assets to build a portfolio of securities, as shown in its prospectus. The mutual fund's objective in the investment category determines the risk.

Mutual funds are investments for investors that build portfolio assets timed in years, not months or weeks. A mutual fund is structured and maintained to achieve the category objectives in the prospectus.

As an investor before investing in a mutual fund, you need to know the current performance, the returns for previous years, the distribution of income and capital gains, and the risk.

Making investments in mutual funds should result in maximizing gains in a positive market and minimizing losses in a negative market. This can best be achieved by a maintaining a diversified retirement portfolio which includes stock /equity mutual funds, Bond funds, and assuming the risk involved.

The moneymaking mutual funds in this paperback consist of stock equity investments. Stock/equity mutual funds purchase securities from companies and industries in the U.S. or foreign stock markets.

The mutual funds are categorized according to company size, the investment style of the holdings in the portfolio and geography. The categories include a vast variety of investments.

Mutual funds are not guaranteed by the U.S. government or FDIC. There are no guarantees of future performance. A healthy and prosperous portfolio is achieved by knowing the annual gains and losses, long-term investment returns, and income/ capital gains distribution. The mutual fund's fees & expenses, minimum standard and IRA purchase, investment policy, and risk are also considerations.

One of the best internet tools available to investors is using a mutual fund's ticker symbol. A unique symbol is assigned to every mutual fund and follows the mutual fund's name. For example, Vanguard Health Care - VGHCX.

Financial search engines provide vital information necessary for investors to make investment decisions. The ticker symbol represents all the company's securities listed, which are used by investors and traders to place trade orders. It also identifies the mutual fund.

No-load (NL) funds are mutual funds that do not charge for purchases. This occurs when investment shares are sold directly by the investment company to the investor, you.

The sales fee charged by mutual funds is called a load. The sales fee can range from 4.00% to 5.75%. Loads represent only one of the fees to consider when investing.

Net Asset Value (NAV): Mutual fund investment price at the investment market closes. Capital gains increase the net asset value at the market closing. Capital losses and stockholder distribution will reduce the net asset value at the market closing.

When mutual funds sell an asset at a larger price than originally purchased, the fund has a capital gain. A capital loss occurs when the asset price of an asset is less than originally paid.

Income/Capital Gains Distribution: Stockholders (investors) receiving mutual fund distributions can receive the proceeds or reinvest the income/capital gains.

IRA assets that are reinvested are not taxable until reaching the age of 72. After that policy, distributions paid to stockholders are taxable.

In a mutual fund selling an investment and the asset held for over a year, the gain or loss is a long-term capital gain or loss.

2022 Best Mutual Funds

Investments held by a mutual fund for less than one year, any gain or loss is a short-term capital gain or loss.

Mutual fund gains and losses are netted together. If the fund has a net gain, the increase is distributed to the stockholder once a year.

By law, mutual funds must pay stockholders out income and realized capital gains. Distributions reduce the net asset value (NAV) by the dollars of the distribution payout.

Dollar-cost-averaging: Investors reinvest mutual fund distributions or purchase investments regardless of whether the market is up or down. The results of these actions are that shares are purchased, and the purchase price (net asset value) can be high or lower.

Listed below is the criterion for money-making mutual funds:

1. Above-average category ranking
2. Above average short & long-term returns
3. No Load fees.
4. Dollar-cost-averaging
5. Distribution of dividends.

When purchasing a mutual fund, a self-directed investor should know the mutual fund investment, such as Managed futures strategy fund A. Call 877-277-6933, ask to request the application to be emailed and return rn the application with a check

Shortly after that, you will receive a confirmation report that includes the trade date, dollar amount, share price (Net Asset Value), and total shares for the transaction.

****

www.ingramcontent.com/pod-product-compliance
Lightning Source LLC
Chambersburg PA
CBHW052359220526
45465CB00003BB/1170